# The Millimetre Game

## Key Strategies for Achieving Your Goals

Marco Kelly

# Table Of Contents

# Introduction

If you have read or listened to any of my work, or attended any of my public speaking engagements, you have likely heard me retell the old African saying which poses the question "How do you eat an elephant?" and answers it with "One bite at a time."

The millimetre game is based on this simple but very profound and relevant philosophy.

We are all driven to achieve something in life. We all have goals or dreams. They could relate to fitness, health, finances, relationships, accomplishments, career or business, etc. The challenge sometimes is that we can very often get in our own way in achieving our goals and dreams. Sometimes it comes down to fears, limiting beliefs, unhealthy assumptions about life or even our own selves, or sometimes it simply comes down to our expectations. Sometimes we expect certain results at a faster pace than is possible in reality due to external forces or limitations.

This book addresses the Expectations Factor in the pursuit of our better selves.

## The Garden Snail

**Getting from Point A to Point B**

In our fast paced world, we are often in a rush to get from point A to Point B. We have developed a deep impatience that permeates almost everything we do in life, to the point that we often have to remind ourselves to slow down and relax.

From this perspective, when we watch a garden snail faced with the task of going from one end of the garden to the other end, it almost seems pointless to us. To go so slow and to take so long seems like a total waste of time. The snail might take five minutes and only move an inch or two.

So, why does it do it? Because it is driven to do it. It does not contemplate the options available, or make the decision to make the journey; it simply does it, like a spider builds a web, or a salmon swims upstream.

But, just like the snail, the spider or the salmon, we are also driven to do something. Maslow covers this in his philosophy of the Hierarchy of Needs. This refers to 5 tiered needs grouping with the bottom tier being our physiological needs like eating, breathing, sleeping, etc. And, let's face it, where any of those needs are in jeopardy, there is nothing else in our minds at the time. If we can't breathe there is nothing else in our minds than getting the next breath. If we are very hungry or very tired, then we think of nothing else than eating or sleeping. My favorite example is standing in the soup aisle at the grocery store, but you have to pee really bad. And because of this intense need to pee, your brain simply does not have the cognitive functioning ability to choose which soup you want.

The second tier of Maslow's Hierarchy is safety and security, things like employment, personal security, resources, etc. Then we have love and belonging, or our social and relationship needs, then Esteem which focuses on things like respect, status, freedom, and the top drive is Self-Actualization: The desire to become the most that one can be.

These are our drives. If we understand these drives fully, you can usually quite quickly identify with someone what drives them by identifying what their most basic unmet need is. It could be social acceptance, or status, a sense of connection.

The key then is in understanding ourselves. What is our most basic unmet need? If our Physiological needs are met, security and safety needs are not an issue, maybe our goal is to develop a meaningful relationship with a partner, or have more friends, or reconnect with our family in a more meaningful way. Perhaps we seek a promotion at work (recognition: level 4) or we want to learn a new language (becoming more: level 5), drive a nice car (Status: Level 4).

One of the key, but strangely often missed, strategies for achieving goals, is to understand what our goals actually are, and what basic need we have that is driving this goal.

Imagine you are in a rowboat. You can row forwards, you can row backwards or you could not row at all. You have the opportunity every day to row in the direction of your goals and dreams. But sometimes we row backwards without even realizing it. And sometimes we aren't even rowing at all.

So, like the garden snail, you need to keep rowing forward. Sure you can take a rest sometimes; sure you can even paddle backwards as long as you are aware and actually choose to move backwards for a bit. But the important thing to know is that everything you do either contributes to your forward momentum, or prevents it.

So like the garden snail, in order to achieve your goals, or get to the other end of the garden, you gotta keep moving forward.

# Behavior Reflects Commitment

Actions and Choices are products of our beliefs and philosophies

Darren went to a personal trainer and the trainer asked Darren what his goals were. Darren replied that he wanted to lose twenty pounds, run a half marathon in May and have more energy.

The trainer replied that those were crappy goals. Darren was a bit shocked by the abrupt stance the trainer was taking. (Pattern interruption)

The trainer continued. He stated that he would recommend a nutrition plan and a weekly exercise regimen and, if Darren stuck to the plan, his rewards would be that he would lose twenty pounds, run a half marathon in May and have more energy.

By reframing the goals, the trainer focused the attention to the steps, rather than the outcome.

If our goal is to fall in love, we can't focus on falling in love. We have to focus on doing the things that create the opportunity for us to meet someone with whom we can fall in love. Those things, then, become the goal, with the reward of developing a long term meaningful relationship with someone we adore, and who adores us.

The challenge however, is that sometimes the long term goal takes a back seat to more immediate wants and desires.

There is a saying used in the Weight Watcher's world that goes: Don't give up what you want the most, for what you want right now.

This is, along with anxiety, one of the most common impediments to the path of self-actualization.

One of the most consistent attributes of very successful people is the ability to delay gratification for the bigger prize.

Have you ever heard of the marshmallow test? For those of you who haven't, the marshmallow test was conducted by Stanford University in 1972 and was performed with kids around the age of 4 or 5. The child is offered a marshmallow or pretzel stick, then told that if they can wait 15 minutes before eating the marshmallow, they will receive a second treat. Then they leave the room and note whether the child eats the one marshmallow and doesn't get the second one, or whether they held out and got the extra treat. Follow up studies to the children from this study concluded that the children who were able to hold out and get the second treat achieved more in life including higher SAT scores, better health and fitness levels and more.

What was determined in this, and subsequent studies, was that the process of delaying gratification was more relevant to suppressive and avoidance mechanisms; the systems the children used to resist the immediate temptation, than some inherent or genetic trait. Granted, some of us may have these traits more inherently, just as some people are inherently better at Math, Music or Sports. However, that does not mean that only by having these inherent advantages can one succeed in these areas. We can develop our own systems to help us resist the temptations of the things we crave now, but which can impede our long term success.

What we can state quite assertively, is that our behavior reflects our commitment.

Jason was sitting in a café once with Dave. Jason is a very strong guy, and is built quite stocky. Jason also has a sweet tooth and enjoys the desserts, which have added a few extra pounds to his midsection. Dave, on the other hand, was ripped. His six-pack was visible even through his shirt.

Jason noticed that a couple of lovely ladies across the room were checking Dave out. Jason is a very jovial fellow, so in a mostly joking manner, made a jab at Dave about his physique in mock jealousy. Dave however responded with a simple statement:

"I guess it's not that important to you."

Jason was taken aback for a second, but asked "What do you mean?"

Dave replied, "If it was that important to you, you'd do something about it."

If it was that important to you, you would do something about it.

There really is no better way to sum up the concept of behavior reflecting commitment.

The other thing we hear a lot is this: I didn't have time.

This, as you probably well know, is an excuse. It's a crock of shit, because, here's the hard dose of reality, we can always find the time to do the things we want to do.

Is it always the case? No. Sometimes we have much bigger priorities and big events happening in our lives for a period of time that makes it very difficult to get in that extra exercise, or read that extra book, or complete those language lessons. But, usually, that's not the case. We spend time doing things like watching YouTube or TikTok videos, watching TV or movies, playing candy crush or Sudoku. And, while there is nothing wrong with doing those things, we have to admit that they are not moving the boat.

Everything we do either moves the boat the direction we want it to go, moves it backwards, or it stops altogether. What can also happen sometimes is that we find ourselves rowing our boat in a different direction.

I've written before about Michelle. Michelle asked me one day how she could make more money. I asked her why she wanted to make more money and she replied that she wanted a better life. She wanted a nice house and a nice car and to be able to travel.

So, I advised Michelle that there are always options available to make more money. Get a better job, work 2 jobs, even 3 jobs, invest her money wisely and build her ability to accomplish those things.

Michelle replied that she helps her sister with her kids, and she spends time with her family, so she doesn't have time to work more jobs.

From this it was obvious what Michelle was committed to. She wanted certain things in her life, but perhaps they really weren't that important to her. What was important to Michelle was her family. Her behavior, spending time with her family and helping her sister with her children, were what Michelle was committed to.

I told Michelle this:

"It seems to me that the things you want are not on the path that you are on. So you have a few options; Change the path you are on to align with the things you want, change the things you want to align with the path you are on, or find another path that compromises the two."

One of the things we often fail to do is ensure that the path we are on aligns with the things we want, and sometimes the things we say we want are not really the things we really want.

Sometimes there is a societal or family expectation to achieve something and so we believe we want that, we tell ourselves and others that we want that, but our behavior does not really reflect a commitment to whatever "that" is.

In many cases, however, the thing we neglect to include in the equation is our self.

You may really want something, it's your goal, your dream, but what you fail to fully acknowledge is that whether you get it or not is not due to some external forces, or by the grace of someone else, it is by your own actions.

One of the most valuable lessons in life that you can learn is to hold yourself accountable for absolutely everything in your life; the good and the bad. Sure, there are external factors, things that happen to you, but you still get to choose how you react to those things. Whether you allow them to beat you or you push through and win.

So, in the pursuit of that thing you want, that life you dream about, or just that new skill or ability or whatever, you have to hold yourself 100% accountable for whether you get it or not.

Sometimes the things we want are on the other side of that which we fear, or which causes anxiety. The average salesman is afraid of cold-calling. The idea of going into a place to try to sell something, to get to know the buyer and know the right questions to ask. What if you get rejected? What if they ask you something to which you don't know the answer? The truth is in that scenario; in the beginning you are going to fail more often than you succeed. Until you learn how to do it better by failing. And then your paradigm shifts and you enjoy it because you are more confident and competent and successful. But you have to push through that ugly stuff in the beginning before you get to the gold on the other side.

In the beginning you are going to be rejected. Sometimes you will be rejected because you think you will be rejected, which has to do with your body language and non-verbal signals you are sending to your prospect. You're going to stumble, stammer, and maybe even fall flat on your face. But once you accept that those things are in the recipe, that they are to be expected, then you face them with a different mindset, than some idealistic impression that you should be able to hit home runs on your first at-bat.

You can't learn to swim, if you don't get in the water.

You can't get better at something, if you aren't willing to fail at it in the beginning.

And this is where the commitment comes in. Are you willing to fight through the tough, ugly beginning, to get to the reward on the other side?

Are you able to push through the fear and anxiety to reap the benefits of overcoming those things?

Sometimes by simply understanding that those things are part of the journey, they no longer carry the same weight.

When I began my first B2B sales job, I was on a drive along with the owner of the company. We pulled up to a building that had a no-soliciting sign on it. I pointed it out. My boss said: "Yeah, it usually takes a new salesperson a few months to get past those."

That simple statement changed the power of that sign for me. It became a hurdle, rather than a road-block. It was no longer something that prevented me from doing what I do, but a personal challenge.

2 weeks into the job I was on my own going around doing cold-calls. I pulled up to a building with one of those signs on it. I parked the car, sat and stared at it for about 5 minutes. Then I said to myself: "Well, if I'm going to get over it someday, it might as well just be today." I got out, went into the building, and made my pitch.

I didn't get the sale. I didn't even do a great pitch. But on the path of the journey of my becoming more, I had a great day. From that point on I barely noticed those signs. They meant nothing to me. Funny, how something that once would have stopped me dead in my tracks was now something I didn't pay any attention to.

Are there any things like that in your life? Things that have power over you, but you need only look at them differently to eliminate any impact it might have on you or your choices?

If there are, and you are either unwilling or incapable of overcoming them, then your next step would be to realize that the path you are on does not lead to those things, and you should then change your path. Just give up on those dreams. Forget about those things you want and accept a life of mediocrity and failure.

Is that what you want? I didn't think so. You wouldn't be reading this book if that is how you felt.

So how do you overcome them? Reframe them. Just like the trainer reframed Darren's "Goals" into "Rewards". Reframe your road-blocks into hurdles.

Accept that struggling in the beginning is part of the recipe. It is a stepping stone on the path to achieving. It is not a roadblock, it is a hurdle. It is a hurdle that you can get over. You can beat this. But you have to stay committed. And you have to be aware, every day, of whether your behavior is moving your boat forward or backwards. Or whether you're just floating in the water and waiting to see which way the current will take you. Because there are many people out there in the world who are just floating. Going where the wind blows them, wishing for a better life, instead of setting goals and plotting paths. Dreaming of the things they want, but never including their own actions, choices and behavior as the crucial ingredients in the recipe for achievement.

Behavior reflects commitment. And every day is an opportunity to move your boat forward, you just gotta row. It's not always easy. In fact, some days you have to fight the currents, you have to row when you're tired. You have to row when you really don't feel like rowing. Want to know a little secret? The single most common attribute among the most successful is this: You do the things you need to do even when you really don't want to do them. This ties in with delayed gratification.

You might want to do something else right now, but that won't be rowing forward.

In the next section, we will address certain specific examples of this. I will highlight certain things, often perceived as road-blocks, and help you to reframe them so that you can see them as hurdles and something to overcome.

# The Millimetre Game

Progress is not a product of one action, but like the erosion of a cliff face, it is the result of cumulative action.

In the pursuit of achievement, it is important to remember that results are often slow, and not immediately noticeable.

This is why I refer to it as The Millimetre Game. Every day of doing something may only gain you a millimetre. But, after 10 days, you gain a centimetre. And then another. And then another, until you've gained a metre, and eventually, if you keep going, a kilometre.

And, like the snail in the garden, it is almost always very slow going.

So, every day you have to look at the day as an opportunity to gain another millimetre.

You get to choose, throughout the day, whether you row that millimetre forward, or don't, or whether you're going to take a backwards day. Which is sometimes ok.

Depending on that thing that you're trying to achieve, it can take a lot out of you to keep rowing forward every single day. And, sometimes you need a break. And, sometimes you need to back a step or even two.

But let those rests be your choice. Own that step back or pause. Don't let it happen because of fear or anxiety. Don't talk yourself into accepting failure because you are having a bad day, or a rough week, or you're unhappy with the perceived lack of progress. Keep pushing on. Take a break if you need it. Press pause and hold for a bit, then get back into it.

Is it likely that the snail rests now and then on the way to the other end of the garden? Absolutely she does. She has to in order to keep the energy up to keep moving forward.

Just don't let the break become the default. Don't let floating in the water, or rowing backwards, become the default.

Let's break down some key goals and common hurdles.

## Fitness

Fitness: The pursuit of well-being, strength, agility, and the ultimate physique. Or perhaps you just don't want to be gassed every time you climb the stairs.

Fitness is a great example of The Millimetre Game. Whether you're looking to lose weight, gain muscle, improve respiratory function, run faster, run longer or jump higher, a focus on exercise and nutrition and a disciplined practice is required. But progress can be slow. You won't see immediate results, but over time, with consistent effort, you will see, and feel, the rewards of your efforts.

To develop a higher level of fitness, whether your focus is on weight management, strength or physical ability, both nutrition and exercise are crucial factors to success. Many experts propose that nutrition contributes about 65% towards results. This means that what you ingest throughout the day plays a vital role in whether you are moving your boat forwards or backwards.

Now, does this mean that you have to eat only eggs, oatmeal, chicken breasts and salads? No. It doesn't.

One could argue that the more of that stuff you eat, the better, but it is not a sustainable practice.

Many experts in nutrition would suggest that you replace the bad things with good things, but that an 80%-90% focus on healthy eating would be best. Does this mean that you can't have a cheat meal? Not at all. In fact cheat meals are often recommended, because deprivation diets have a history of failure.

To look at nutrition and exercise as a combined effort is key. When you eat you consume calories, and you consume Macro and Micronutrients. Let's look at Macro Nutrients for a second.

Macro Nutrients are Proteins, Fats and Carbs.

Proteins are essential for protein synthesis which is the building of lean body mass. Increasing your lean body mass improves your body's ability to burn calories at rest, and aids in physical ability.

Fats, more specifically the healthy fats such as monounsaturated or polyunsaturated fats, are essential for the body's vital functions and health. They help fight inflammation, lower blood pressure, help fight heart disease by lowering bad cholesterol and increase good cholesterol and more.

Carbohydrates provide the units of fuel for the body. All carbohydrates, regardless of where they come from, are converted into glucose which the body uses for fuel. What is not used, is stored as fat.

So, in deciding your ratios of macronutrients, it is important to remember that all 3 of them are essential. If you are looking at increasing lean body mass, you need to consume proteins.

Fats have 9 calories for each gram, to the 4 calories that proteins and carbs have per gram, so it is generally important to limit fats appropriately. It is important to focus on what types of fatty acids you are consuming. Good fats like polyunsaturated or monounsaturated fats are good for you, and bad fats like Trans fats and many saturated fats are bad for you. But not all saturated fats are bad for you. Dairy fat is actually good for you, as is coconut oil, which is lauric acid, which is amazing for you. But stay away from Trans fats and bad oils like palm oil.

Carbs are vital for energy, unless you have switched to a ketone energy system, where you use fats as fuel instead of carbs.

The important thing to remember about calories in your pursuit of becoming the best version of you is that you want each calorie to bring with it as many good friends as possible. What this refers to is the micro nutrients. Vitamins and minerals your body needs for healthy functioning.

When we consume empty calories, we miss out on key opportunities to provide good fuel for our bodies. Think of your body like the engine of a car. You need fuel and you need oil. But think about the fuel for a second. If you were given the option to choose between a clean fuel that helped you engine operate at optimum performance, or a fuel that impeded your engines ability to perform well, which would you choose? This is the choice you make every single day with food. Empty calories have little to no nutritional benefit. Like alcohol, candy or highly processed foods.

Does this mean you can never have a drink, or eat candy or processed foods? Not at all. But you get to choose how far backwards you want to row your boat.

Knowing that by eating more vegetables and nutrient dense natural foods you are fueling your body with everything it needs to perform well. So by doing this, you are rowing your boat forward towards your fitness goals. Drinking excessive alcohol or eating too much candy, would essentially be rowing your boat backwards.

In addition, eating empty calories, or drinking too much alcohol, could negate any progress you might otherwise have made with any exercise. It is important to note as well, especially where you may be looking to diminish your fat stores and increase lean body mass, that your liver will always prioritize cleaning out alcohol toxins before getting to oxidizing fats that you are burning.

So, eating clean and exercising, and understanding the factors that contribute to, or impede, your progress, is important to understanding the path that you are on, and whether or not, it actually leads to things you want.

If you want to be fit and healthy, but eat poorly, don't choose well the foods you consume, and drink too much alcohol, it would be safe to say that your goals and your path are not in alignment. And, the key factor in this is YOU. YOUR choices, YOUR actions, YOUR behavior. And you have to ask yourself, what does my behavior suggest about my commitment to my goals?

So, yes, you will be tempted. You will have cravings. You will not feel like working out, or going for that run, or walk, or whatever form of exercise you have chosen. But remember. It is a Millimetre Game and every day is an opportunity to move forward. If you choose to not do the things you need to do to move forward, you simply do not move forward.

So every day you need to remind yourself of the commitment to your goals, eliminate as many temptations as you can, and delay the immediate gratification, push through those tough times when you really don't feel like moving your ass, and you will move that millimetre. And that Millimetre may at times seem insignificant, but like the erosion of that cliff face, it is the result of cumulative action.

I have a weakness for chocolate. So I don't keep any in the house. Does that mean I never eat chocolate? Not a chance. I still want a life worth living, don't I? I used to pick up a chocolate bar every time I went to the grocery store and eat it in the car on the drive home. Now I only do it maybe once a month. I allow myself that little pause, or slight row backwards. But do I look at them every time I go to the store and think about it? Every. Single. Time. But I force myself to remember the millimetres and which way I want them to go. I remind myself of my goal and hold myself accountable for whether I move forward or backward, and I remind myself to not give up that which I want the most, for what I want right now.

I turned 50 last year. My Instagram name is 6packat50. Because that was my goal. To have a six-pack when I turned 50. Did I get there? Not quite. You can see the outlines, and my obliques are clearly visible, but it isn't what I would call a six-pack. Does that mean that now I have turned 50 that I stopped trying? Not at all. It's still my goal, and I'm still pushing forward. Do I have backwards days? Absolutely.

But I keep pushing, and I keep my eye on the path and ensure that it is aligned with my goal. And I remember that it is a Millimetre Game. I may not be at the end of the garden yet, but I know with absolute certainty, that if I keep moving forward, I will get there.

Other examples

I'm not going to keep digging into this, as I am sure you get it by now and I'm trying to keep this book short. But I will highlight a few other areas and common examples of where the Millimetre Game is important.

Finances

Personal Finance encompasses a lot of different factors including earnings, budgets, spending and investments.

Earnings is a key one because many people feel that they do not have any control over their earnings. It is dependent on the choices that other people make about them. I propose that this is absolutely false.

I'll share with you a lesson my father taught me at a very young age: If you are making 5 dollars per hour, work like you are making 20.

Why? Build your value to the organization. Increase your worth within the organization and they will pay you more. If you wait to be paid more to do more, it'll never happen.

Would you pay more for something and then see if it performs better? Or do you need to see proof of its superior performance before you would pay the extra money? Well, your value is no different.

Earnings can also be tied to additional sources of income or starting your own business.

Accept that your earnings are tied to the choices you make and learn what other choices you have available to you.

Budgets are crucial for managing finances. Just like with Fitness, where you need to know your calories in and your calories out, with finances you have to have an intimate understanding of every dollar in and every dollar out. Eliminate unnecessary spending and put money aside before you do anything else. Get addicted to seeing your savings grow and learn to make do with less.

Spending is usually the pursuit of immediate gratification. Again we need to evaluate the goal you want the most, to whatever shiny new thing that is that has caught your eye.

But remember the Millimetre Game. Get rich quick schemes are rare and usually shady or unethical. It is possible to develop some new technology, or have a brilliant idea that has huge growth potential. And you might have the key to the next big thing. But don't hang your hat on that.

Develop good finance habits and know that for the most part, your wealth grows slowly. A few dollars put aside every week can add up over time. But not putting aside a few dollars every week will never add up to anything.

Investments are crucial if you want your money to go to work to make more money. There is risk here, but you can usually mitigate risks by involving specialists to help you. But you can't invest money, if you aren't saving money. So the millimetre game can work for you and you can accelerate the game by investing your money wisely. It's still a millimetre game. Don't expect to retire in a year. But play the long game and you'll be cruising around the Caribbean in your golden years. It is possible to fare better than the average, and there are things you can do to yield greater outcomes, but they all involve delayed gratification and playing the millimetre game.

Accomplishments

I stated earlier that you can't learn to swim if you don't get into the water. There really isn't anything that you can achieve without doing the groundwork.

If you want to learn to play an instrument, it requires an immense amount of practice. Learning a language requires an immense amount of time learning vocabulary and tenses and conjugations.

If you want to learn to sail, or surf, or fly a plane, or jump out of planes, or get a black belt in Taekwondo. Anything. It takes time.

This highlights the millimetre game very well.

Learning to play the guitar has a number of steps including learning the frets, the fingering, the scales, the chords, picking techniques, strumming techniques, rhythm patterns, up strokes and down strokes. And then, if you're looking to play and sing, you gotta figure out how to do all of that while you're singing a melody in pitch and tune and rhythm with the song you're playing.

It's amazing when you get there, and you do have small little rewards along the way. But it is a journey; a path to becoming a musician, even if it's just a hobby. Something you've always wanted to do. Then the question is: how committed are you to this goal? Are you willing to put in the time to practice? One of my best friends is a brilliant musician and he taught me this simple little rule: IF you practice 5 minutes a day, you'll sound like you practice 5 minutes a day. IF you practice 8 hours a day, then you'll sound like you practice 8 hours a day. Then, the only question is: what do you want to sound like. And this is entirely your choice. It is up to you.

If you want to learn to speak Japanese, the same rule applies. It is the Millimetre Game of learning vocabulary and context and pronunciation and more. And this requires practice.

But it is important to remember that it is a millimetre game. There is an old Arabic saying that translates to: "No-one was born a teacher." We all have to learn the things we want to be good at. But if you're not willing to put in the time to learn the things you need to learn to become good at the thing you want to become good at, then you're really only wasting your time. And you, little snail, will never get to the end of the garden.

So, you have to set little goals for yourself. Your goal becomes a certain amount of practice every day, so that every day you move your boat a millimetre. Your goal becomes reading and learning and watching videos that relate to the things you want to learn so you can help yourself accelerate your millimetre game.

# Summary

Sitting on the couch is easy. But sitting on the couch produces no results.

If you want results, you have to take action. But don't get discouraged when you don't see amazing results right away. It takes time; one millimetre a day or sometimes even less than that. But a quarter of a millimetre is better than no millimetre at all. It's still moving forward. Maybe one day you'll move 2 millimetres.

And there will be days when you go back a millimetre, or even 2 or more.

But as long as you are pushing forward, you'll get back on track and make those up.

I recently had a conversation with myself about my own journey. I had to remind myself that there wasn't a race. Not to blow my brains out with unrealistic expectations. It's a millimetre game. The only thing I can ever ask of myself is that I am focused on moving forward.

I will stumble. I will fall down. I will sometimes fail. But that is all part of the process of getting better. Sometimes I need a break and I take one, but I remind myself that the break cannot become the norm. I remind myself that the progress I have made today may have only been a small drop in the bucket, but when I add in the drops from the days before and the days ahead, I know I can, and will, fill that bucket.

Sometimes it will be very hard to move your boat. Some days it will seem almost impossible. Do you when it feels impossible the most? When you haven't moved it in a while.

Whenever I stay on a consistent weekly exercise plan, some days are hard, but for the most part I get in and get it done. But after an injury, when I've been off for a while, getting back into working out is the hardest thing to do.

So when I am in the weekly plan, I fight to stay in the weekly plan. Days might get thrown off, I might be travelling, or my day gets thrown because of a customer crisis, but I make it up, or reset and start again the next day or so. I know I can't take too much time off, because then lethargy sets in and I will start finding every excuse under the sun to not do what I know I absolutely need to do in order to keep my boat moving.

But whenever I am at my most weakest, I ask and answer these questions:

Do I really want this? YES

Am I committed?  YES

Am I willing to do whatever it takes? YES

Then I say to myself:

Then get your ass up and show it!!

Behavior reflects commitment. Words don't mean shit, and excuses don't produce results.

I know it's a millimetre game, and every day is an opportunity to move forward.

Cease the day!!

Thank you for reading.

www.ingramcontent.com/pod-product-compliance
Lightning Source LLC
Chambersburg PA
CBHW020942160726
47993CB00007B/2899